AF433301

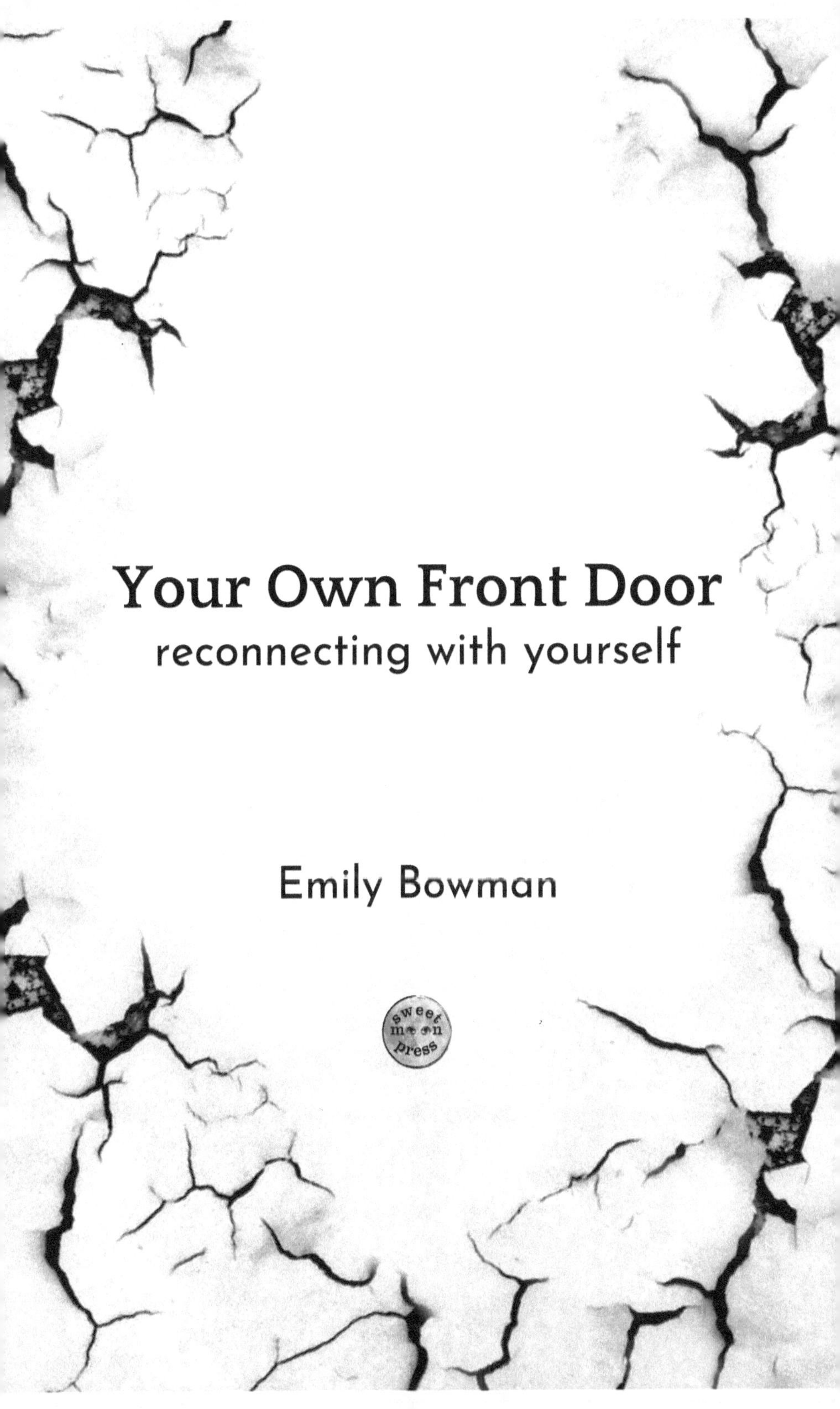

Your Own Front Door

reconnecting with yourself

Emily Bowman

sweet moon press

Contents

Contents (cont.)

Contents (cont.)

Contents (cont.)

When you arrive
at your own front door,
led by the torch of a truth
you forgot to remember,
guided by whatever spark
burns boldest inside you,
just stand there, soothed
by the recognition
of your own essence...

-from the poem,
"Your Own Front Door"
by Emily Bowman

Introduction

Welcome to the path to your own front door! Whatever inkling of intuition led you to this book, or whichever kind person in your life shared this book with you, I'm so glad you are here, and so glad you are open to the process of connecting with yourself in a deeper way so that you can live a more intentional life.

"I don't even know who I am," is something I've heard many clients say throughout my years as a therapist. I've also heard friends and family members say it, and I've seen people post about it on social media. It can be so easy to wander away from ourselves as we fulfill roles in jobs, relationships, families, etc. Because these roles are important, and because we often have multiple roles to fulfill at once, it can be so easy to let our relationships with ourselves take a backseat while we focus time and energy on maintaining relationships with others and with the work we do in the world. If we have caretaking roles in our families and/or if our work involves helping others, it is even more likely we will get absorbed by those roles and will, eventually, stop nourishing the connection to our own spirits. Ultimately, this disconnection can negatively impact our work, our relationships, our health, and more.

The first step in finding your way back to yourself is to recognize that you might have gotten a little lost or gotten buried under the obligations in your life. Sometimes this can be hard to recognize on your own, and you may not even realize it until someone in your life gives you feedback that you just don't seem like yourself anymore, or someone who has known you at an earlier time in your life reminds you about things that have been unique and defining characteristics of who you are. Please note, the disconnection to which I'm referring goes beyond the typical changing and evolving tastes and preferences we all experience throughout our lives, and I am also not referring to the healthy and necessary behavior changes we sometimes make on our paths of growth as we leave destructive habits behind. The disconnection I'm referring to involves feeling disconnected with the essence of who you are and not really feeling like you know yourself anymore.

There are a few signs that might let you know you've strayed a little from your connection with yourself. Some of those signs are:

- Feeling exhausted and/or burnt out
- Having trouble making decisions
- Feeling disconnected in relationships with others
- Feeling "empty"
- Feeling depressed

- "Numbing out" with mindless and/or addictive behaviors
- Feeling bored
- Feeling like you are in a never-ending rut
- Feeling irritable
- Having a sense that life has no meaning
- Not knowing what to do with down time or days off

If any of this resonates with you, please know that you are not alone, and please know that you can get back to who you really are so you can live a more fulfilling and authentic life. So, how do you even begin finding your way back to yourself? Great question! You are basically becoming a detective looking for clues and information that can lead you to the trail that will take you to what I like to call "your own front door."

Making lists and/or journaling can be a great place to start. The different categories and questions in this book can be springboards and provide inspiration for your lists. The book is designed so that you can write directly in it if you choose. If you prefer a different format, however, you can simply use the categories and questions as prompts to create your own style of lists in your journal, phone, etc.

After much debate internally, and after seeking feedback from several others, I have decided to leave the journaling sections blank instead of lined so that you have more freedom to format your lists and thoughts any way you want, and so that you can add pictures or anything else you choose. I realize some of you (possibly many of you!) prefer lines in your journaling process, and I would encourage you to draw in your own lines if that makes the process easier for you.

If writing isn't really your thing, you can also spend some time reflecting on the list prompts and notice what surfaces, or you can use them as part of a meditation practice. You can also use the prompts in conversations with people who have known you throughout your life to start to get them to provide you with feedback and missing pieces. Making collages can also be a great way to explore some of these aspects of yourself. You could even start a collage book with a different page for each list, and search through magazines and/or old photos for images that jump out at you in response to the different questions.

However you choose to do this work of connecting with yourself, I would encourage you to approach it with curiosity and openness. Know that there are no "wrong" answers...this is just you gathering information about you! There is also no "right" or "wrong" way to use this book. Some of you may want to go through it in a linear way, contemplating and working on one list at a time, while others may find it more useful to start with he category that feels most compelling and jump around, working on several lists at once. However you choose to start your lists, it will probably be most beneficial to keep them open and add to them as you discover more and more information about yourself, and as your tastes, preferences, beliefs, priorities, desires, etc. change over time.

Look back over your lists regularly to celebrate how much you're learning and to reflect on the growth and progress you're making on this journey. It might also help to share your learning and growth with a friend or family member or therapist. Sharing can help hold you accountable for living in a more intentional way that aligns you with who you are and who you want to be.

Above all, have fun with this process and don't take it (or yourself!) too seriously; at the end of the day, you're just gathering information, and maybe, just maybe, it might help you find your way back to your own front door! Enjoy the journey!

Getting Acquainted

Let's get to know **you** and some of the basic things that may already be part of your awareness of who you are.

What I Already Know
about Who I Am

Start by listing all the things you already know about yourself...physical characteristics, personality traits, things you do, things you don't do, things you won't do, things you love, things you hate, etc. Don't censor, don't edit, just write until you run out of things to write.

Roles I Play/Hats I Wear

Think about all the different roles you play and hats you wear throughout your day, week, month, etc. These can be related to your relationships and your job, and they can also be related to the things you do to try to keep your life and the lives of the people around you running smoothly. Some might be roles you participate in willingly, and some might be roles you really don't want but find yourself in anyway. The big ones will be obvious (parent, sibling, spouse, job title, etc.), but think about the more subtle ones too (dogwalker, grocery getter, spider killer, plant waterer, listener, motivator, tear soaker-upper, etc.).

Look through your list of roles. Circle all the roles that you want to keep and put stars by the roles that are most important to you. If there are any roles you don't especially enjoy and don't want to keep, it might be helpful to spend some time brainstorming ways that you might be able to delegate and/or establish boundaries around, or perhaps even eliminate.

Feedback from Others

Think about feedback you've gotten about yourself throughout your life from friends, teachers, coaches, family members, romantic partners, etc. Some of it might feel really good and some of it might make you cringe because it's about things you don't really love about yourself. This is a chance to lay it all out on the table...the good, the bad, and the ugly. Even if you don't agree 100% with the feedback, write it all down. These are clues to the ways others perceive you, AND this is also a chance to evaluate whether what others have told you may not be true about you at all. Either way, it's valuable information as you dive deeper into connecting with who you are.

Look through your list. Circle the feedback you agree with and put a rectangle around feedback you don't. Reflect on the feedback you agree with and contemplate whether it is something you might want to change. You may also want to spend some time reflecting on the feedback you don't agree with, and explore whether it might reflect a blind spot you have about yourself and/or if it might be more a reflection of others' life experiences shaping their perceptions of you.

Things I Like about Myself

Ooooo, this one might be tricky for some of you. When I ask clients what they like about themselves, they usually squirm and look away and wish the couch would swallow them up so they don't have to answer. Some of you may have been socialized to believe that it's bragging to think about yourself in a positive way, let alone to list out the things you like about yourself. Others may be so focused on the things you don't like that you genuinely cannot come up with anything you like. Do your best to set all of that aside here, and just write whatever comes to mind when you hear the question, "What do you like about yourself?" Even if you're only able to come up with one item in your list to start with, it's a great start, and hopefully this will be a list that grows and grows as you learn more about yourself.

Things I Don't So Much Like about Myself

Sadly, this list is usually easier to fill than the previous one about what you DO like about yourself. Some of you might wonder why I would put this question in here instead of staying with a more positive focus. Knowing the things you don't like about yourself can be really helpful a) in helping you learn more about the WHOLE picture of yourself, and b) in identifying more clearly things you want to work on either changing or accepting about yourself. With that said, please do your best to respond to this prompt in a way that feels constructive instead of in a way that just feels like you're beating yourself up.

Look through your list. First, ask yourself for each item whether this is something that is actually true about you now or if it's a story you've been telling yourself based on something somebody said or experiences you've had earlier in your life. Second, write a 'C' next to everything on the list that is possible to change. Third, circle everything with a 'C' that you are willing to change. If you want to take this even further, choose one of the things you are willing to change about yourself , and then identify a small step you could take toward changing it within the next week.

Talents/Skills/Gifts

Think about any talents, skills, or gifts that you recognize in yourself or that others have identified in you. What are you good at doing? What are some of your traits and characteristics that make you stand out? What types of things come easily to you? What skills have you developed throughout your life? These don't have to be earth-shattering, record breaking, expert-level things! Maybe you're a good listener or a fast learner. Maybe you make really good soft-boiled eggs or maybe you can take apart a washing machine and put it back together without looking at the instruction manual. Be thoughtful with this list, and really let yourself explore ALL your many talents, skills, and gifts.

Look through your list. Are there any skills, talents, or gifts that you're not currently using in your life, but you'd like to? Explore what might be keeping you from using them, and brainstorm some ways you might be able to bring them into your life.

*All that power,
all that radiance,
all that light
you know you have
coiled inside of you,
feel it,
own it,
shine it.
Step into your strength
and use your voice
to say no,
to say yes,
so that everyone
around you knows exactly
who you are,
and there can be absolutely
no excuse for being
anything less.*

-"Accountability"
by Emily Bowman

A Few of My Favorite Things

This section will allow you to think about some of your favorite things. While these lists will likely not involve as much thought and deep searching as some of the other lists in this book, they are still very important in the process of connecting with yourself, and can allow you to be more thoughtful in your choices.

My Favorite Places

Think about places you've been throughout your life. Which ones stand out to you? Which places do you want to return to? Think too about places in your current life that are meaningful to you. These could be specific rooms in your home, restaurants or shops in your town, trails you like to hike, etc. If you're having trouble coming up with favorite places or you notice that you don't have many places you go in your current life, you might challenge yourself to explore some of the places around you, and hopefully you'll find some to add to your list. Choosing to spend more time in your favorite places can be a great way to live a more intentional and fulfiilling life.

My Favorite Movies

Regardless of whether you're a movie buff who's watched thousands of movies or you tend to watch movies only a few times a year, there are likely movies you've watched throughout your life that stand out to you. This list is for the movies that have made you laugh, have made you cry, have made you mad, have inspired you, or have just plain brought you joy.

Once you've made your list, go back through for each movie and think about what it was about that movie that impacted you. Maybe you identified with the theme or one of the characters, maybe it made you think about things a different way, maybe you watched it with a special person or during an impactful time of your life, maybe it made you feel deeply, or maybe it was simply a great movie.

My Favorite Books

You may be an avid reader who reads several books a month or you may have only read books when you had to for school. Either way, there are likely books that have stood out to you as meaningful. Maybe you related to the characters, maybe it let you escape, maybe it inspired you in some way, maybe it taught you something. Think about all the books you've read or listened to throughout your life, and write down the ones that stand out to you.

Once you've identified your list of books, think about what it w
about each book that impacted you. Maybe you identified wit
the theme or one of the characters, maybe it made you thin
about things a different way, maybe you read it, during an
impactful time of your life, maybe it made you feel deeply,
maybe it was simply a great story.

My Favorite Quotes

The words of others can be powerful sources of inspiration and can guide our lives in different ways. Think about quotes you've heard throughout your life that have stuck with you or that have been meaningful to you in some way. Sometimes it can be hard to remember quotes, and if you're having trouble thinking of any, you might be able to remind yourself by looking through a book of quotes or doing a Google search for "popular quotes", "famous quotes" or even search for quotes about specific topics. Also, quotes don't have to be famous or from somebody famous to be powerful. Maybe your aunt or your third grade teacher or your high school soccer coach or your first boss gave you advice or had specific sayings you still remember.

Once you've identified quotes that have been meaningful to you, pick a few of them that are especially meaningful, motivational, inspirational, etc. and put them on sticky notes to hang in your house or car. You could also put them somewhere in your phone so you can look at them regularly, or create a piece of art or make a t-shirt or get a tattoo...the possibilities are endless!

My Favorite Songs

Music can be a great way to connect with yourself. Think about the songs you're listening to now, and songs that have been important to you throughout your life. It could even be a fun exercise to make a timeline and try to remember what songs you were listening to over and over again throughout the different eras of your life.

You might already have some sort of playlist or mix tape with all your favorite songs, but if you don't, it could be a fun project to make a compilation of all the songs that have been part of your path...kind of like the soundtrack to your life story!

*At the intersection of regret
and anticipation sits now--this moment,
this life--waiting for you
to grab it with both hands,
hold it to your chest and feel its pulse
throbbing against yours,
spelling out in capital letters
the invitation to your destiny.*

*And if you choose to accept it,
you choose life, choose big, bold steps
into the unknown, a fierce surrender
of your spirit, a release of all those doubts
you've stockpiled just in case,
all those shoulds that snared you
with their prickly barbs, all those times
you said yes when you meant no,
or no when you meant yes, not realizing
that the only word that matters
is the one you say right now.*

-"And What Will You Say?"
by Emily Bowman

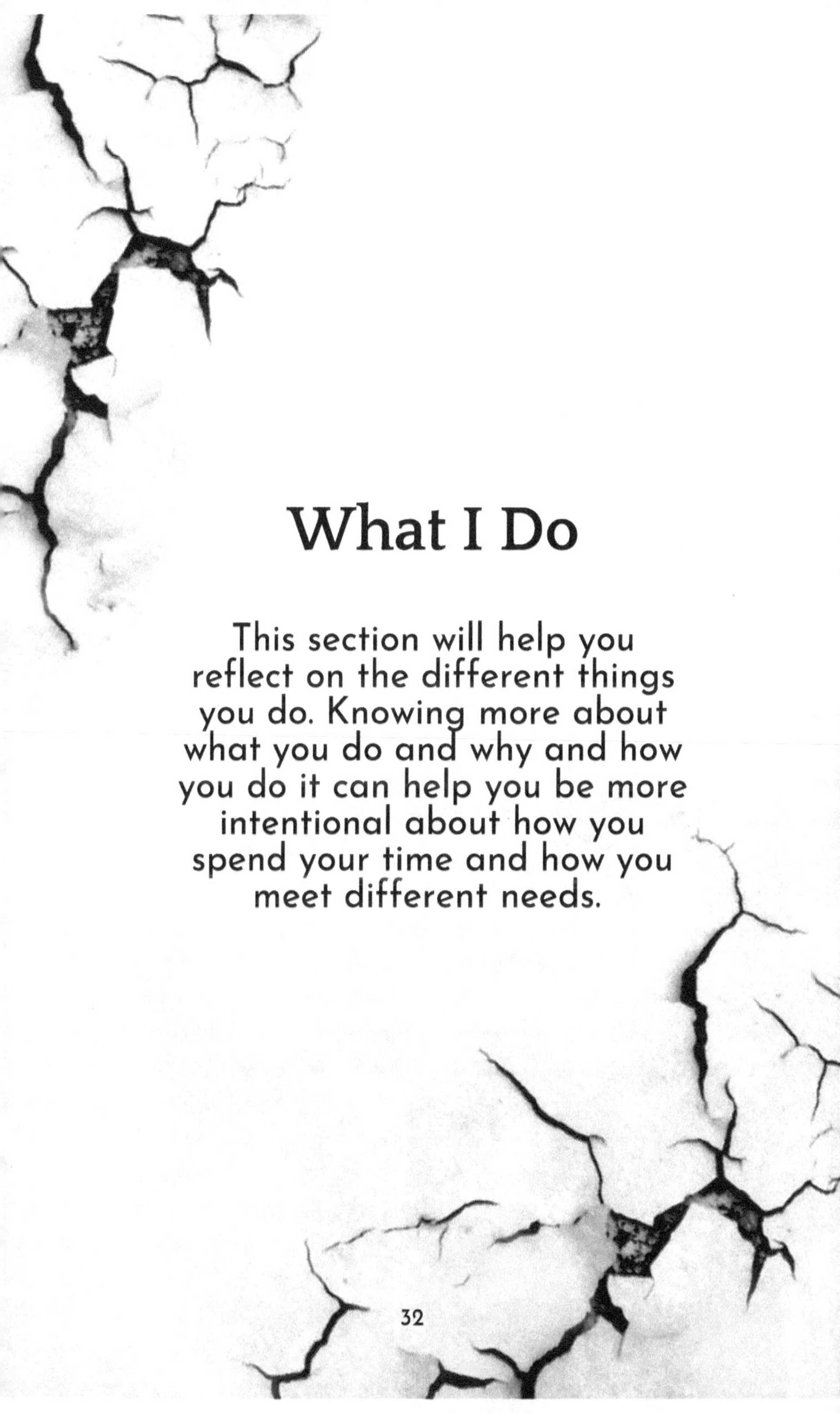

What I Do

This section will help you reflect on the different things you do. Knowing more about what you do and why and how you do it can help you be more intentional about how you spend your time and how you meet different needs.

Things I Really Like to Do

This list is pretty simple and straightforward. What do you really like to do? What kinds of things do you choose to do when you have a choice about what you do? Think about things you like to do in your current life, and think back to things you've liked to do at different stages of your life.

Once you've developed your list, look it over and note how often you do the things you really like to do. Whether you do them often or hardly at all, this can be great information, and can help you make decisions about how you spend your time from this point forward. You might also challenge yourself to choose one or two things you haven't done in a while and find a way to do them this month.

Ways That I Create

Typically people associate the word "create" with artistic pursuits. While artistic pursuits are definitely a form of creating, there are so many more ways to create. Some of you might be thinking, "But I'm not creative", and I would argue that we are all creative in some way. Just because you don't paint or sculpt or write poetry doesn't mean you're not creative. Creativity can manifest itself in grand ways like writing an entire opera, or it can be as simple as saying something funny in a conversation. Creating can also take the form of cooking, baking, building a bookshelf, building a house, building a business, doing a puppet show with children, gardening, writing someone a thoughtful birthday greeting, doodling during a meeting, and SO much more. Basically, creating is simply the act of bringing something into being that was not there before.

Spend some time with this list and really explore all the ways you create. This will likely be a list that you come back to many times as you are struck with realizations about different ways you create or as you experiment with new ways of creating.

Once you have identified ways that you create, think about the things that tend to spark your creativity. Do you feel more creative when you're alone or surrounded by people? Do you create best in silence or with background noise? Do you feel more creative when your life is busy and full or when you have periods of rest and stillness? Do certain songs or seasons or people or moods tend to spark your creativity?

Ways That I Play

Play. This is something most of us do not do as often as we'd like to or need to. Before you start your list, think about what play means to you. It could mean going to a park and swinging or going down the slide, it could mean a game of football or frisbee or rummy, it could mean dancing or singing at the top of your lungs, and it could even mean spinning round and round on the swivel chair in your office when nobody's watching. Basically, play is anything you do that lets you have fun, and it also usually involves a sense of freedom and, sometimes, even a sense of rebellion. As children, play was the language we spoke, and it was the way we moved through the world. Most of us tend to lose our tendency to play as we age, but play is a great way to connect to yourself (and the people around you if you include them!). If you're having trouble connecting to your sense of playfulness and what it might look like in your life, spend some time watching children and let them teach you what it means to play. It can also be helpful to list the ways that you played when you were a child and to notice what type of play you most enjoyed (using your imagination, playing with toys, building/creating things, games, sports, etc.). These can be very helpful clues in figuring out what kinds of play you might enjoy as an adult.

Once you've identified what play means to you, start listing all the ways that you play, big and small. This is another list that will hopefully grow longer and longer over time as you find more ways to incorporate play into your life.

In addition to your list of ways that you play, it can be helpful to start another list about ways you **want** to play, and you can have a lot of fun working your way through the items on that list.

Ways That I Rest

As with the list about play, it might be helpful before you start this list to think about what rest means to you. For some people it means anything they do when they're not working at a job, and for others it means being completely still with no distractions. Once you've identified how you define rest, begin listing all the ways that you give yourself rest.

If you tend to struggle with making time to rest or if you feel guilty about resting, maybe you could begin with a list of things you could do if you had time to rest or gave yourself permission to rest. And please know that knowing more about your relationship to rest is just another way that you are getting to know yourself better, and that this is something you can change if you decide you want to change it.

Ways That I Contribute to the World

Just in case you're thinking that you don't have anything to put on this list, please know that we all contribute to the world in some way (usually many ways!), and every contribution counts. You don't have to win a Nobel Prize or be a firefighter or a pediatric heart surgeon to make the world a better place. Maybe you pick up trash when you see it, maybe you bring humor into heavy situations, maybe you're tall enough to get things off the top shelf for others at the grocery store, maybe you pet lonely cats on the sidewalk, or maybe your smile makes others smile. The "world" can be anybody, any creature, any place, any situation, and whether you realize it or not, you have the power to impact these things, often in very simple ways.

With that in mind, start writing all the ways you contribute to the world, and if you get stuck, your family, friends, and co-workers will probably be able to give you many examples.

As you look at your list, notice any feelings that come up. You might feel surprised at all the ways you contribute. You might feel overwhelmed at the impact you actually have on the world. You might feel disappointed because your list isn't as long as you'd like it to be. The great thing about this list is that starting from this point forward, you have complete control over how long or how short it is. Every day you have multiple opportunities to impact the world in a positive way, and this list can inspire you to be more intentional in whether or not you take those opportunities.

Habits

Our habits, whether they are big or small, helpful or unhelpful, impact many aspects of our lives. They can impact how we spend our time, how we spend our money, how others perceive us, how we think and feel about ourselves, and they can even impact our physical health. This section allows you to look more closely at your habits so that you can be more aware of what serves you and what does not serve you, and so that you can have a clearer idea of behaviors you may want to change as you move forward.

Habits I Like
and Want to Keep

You can start this section with this list of habits you like, or you can flip the page and start with the ones you don't so much like. You can also flip back and forth between the two lists as you think about your habits, in general. It's typically a lot easier to identify the habits we don't like than the ones that we do, and we don't often conceptualize the healthy and constructive behaviors or parts of our routines as habits. They are definitely habits, though, and this is your chance to think about and list all of the habits/routines you've developed that you actually like and that serve you well.

Habits I Don't Like and Want to Change

This list is for the habits that maybe aren't serving you so well. These could be things that take up too much of your time, cost you money you'd rather spend on other things, harm your health, or interfere with your job and/or your relationships. As you make this list, try to be gentle with yourself and have compassion for yourself by recognizing that every habit began simply as a way to meet some sort of need, and that, at the end of the day, we're all just trying to get our needs met one way or another. The wonderful thing about this list is that it will allow you to see that some of the things that used to be helpful in some way are no longer helpful, and that you have a choice about whether or not you want to continue doing them, as well as a choice about meeting your needs in more effective ways.

Note: If any of your habits have become addictive behaviors that you are having a hard time stopping on your own, it may be helpful to reach out to a support group and/or to a professional who specializes in treating addictions.

To take this a little further, next to each habit you put on this list, it might be helpful to note the need it originally met or the purpose it originally served for you. Then for each need/purpose you can ask yourself if it is still a need or purpose needing to be served, and, if it is, whether there might be a more effective way to meet that need or serve that purpose.

Enjoy the possibility of imperfection,
the possibility that you
just might be the you
you try so hard to hide...
the messy, the flabby, the flawed,
the don't-have-it-all-figured-out...
explore the too much, the not enough,
and release expecations
that aren't yours to carry.
Allow and accept mistakes
and not-so-shining moments,
remembering that the possibility
of perfection is, quite simply,
impossible.

-."Grace"
by Emily Bowman

My Relationships

Connection with others is a fundamental human need, and we all fulfill it in different ways. This section allows you to explore your experiences with the relationships in your life and your needs in relationships, both of which can help you understand more about yourself, and can, ultimately, help you have more fulfilling relationships.

Important Relationships

Think about the people and animals who are important to you in your life currently (in a later list you'll get to explore all the people who have been important to you throughout your life). These don't have to be people you see regularly, and they don't even have to be people with whom you interact on a deep level. Include on this list anyone in your current life who is important to you in some way.

Once you've created your list, look through it and think about how much time and energy you put into the relationships with each of the people on your list. Maybe the time/energy you invest in each of these relationships feels right to you, or maybe you want to invest more or less time/energy. This is just information you can use to guide any adjustments you might feel compelled to make.

People I Trust

You may have hundreds of people in your life and only trust a handful of them, or you may have a small circle of people and trust them all. You may also trust different people for different things. This list is a chance to explore and identify who you trust and for what. It may be helpful to break it into a few separate categories of trust (i.e., people you trust to keep secrets, people you trust to do what they say they will do, people you trust to be there for you in a crisis, people you trust to stand up for you, etc). Think about all the different ways you trust people, create your list categories, and then just write whoever comes to mind for each of the lists.

This might stir up some thoughts and feelings about trust, in general, and it can be a great opportunity to reflect on your experiences with trusting others. Look over your lists and notice in which categories you tend to place more or less trust in people. Think back through your life about the experiences you've had with trusting others and how you've learned your lessons about trust. If this feels like a significant issue you want to explore further and/or if there have been traumatic experiences that significantly impact your ability to trust others, it may be helpful to talk to a therapist or other professional who can help guide you through this process.

Things That Are Important to Me in a Friendship

Reflect on friendships you've had throughout your life. What made them meaningful? What things worked for you and what things didn't? What qualities or characteristics are important to you in a friend? What are your needs in friendships?

Things That Are Important to Me in a Romantic Relationship

Reflect on romantic relationships you've had throughout your life. What made them meaningful? What things worked for you and what things didn't? What qualities or characteristics are important to you in a romantic partner? What are your needs in romantic relationships? What are things that romantic partners have done that you really liked? What are things that you really didn't like?

Unfurl
everything wild
and weird
you've hidden
within you,
allowing it
(at last)
to beautify
the world.

-"Unfurl""
by Emily Bowman

My Style

Your style is one of the ways you display who you are. It manifests in the ways you present yourself to the world through what you wear and through how you decorate your living space. For the lists in this section, you might find it easier to make collages or other visual compilations than written lists (although written lists are certainly fine!). Regardless of how you choose to do it, it could be helpful to look through photographs of yourself to see certain patterns in what you tend to wear or what your living spaces have looked like, as well as magazines/online shops to notice what styles tend to grab your attention.

What I Wear

This is a list to help you identify how you express yourself through your clothing, accessories, jewelry, hairstyles, etc. What you wear can be one of the ways you express yourself to the world, and it can be done as simply or as overtly as you choose and as your circumstances allow. Your innate style may have been stifled as a child or adolescent by your family, your school, or your religious or other institutions, or you may be currently struggling with restrictions on what you wear for a number of reasons. Regardless of any internal and external barriers to dressing how you want to dress, I would encourage you to at least take some time to explore how you would dress if you could wear anything you want.

You may know right away what your style is, but if you need a little help, consider the following questions: What types of clothing do you tend to wear most often? Do you prefer patterns or plain colors? What hairstyles/hair colors have you had throughout your life? What colors and fabrics are you drawn toward? Are you more flashy or more understated? Do you keep up with trends or do you have more of a classic style? What types of clothing/accessories/hairstyles do you tend to compliment others on?

Once you've identified your style, play around with it and see if there are things you want to change. Sometimes it can be fun to dress in a completely different way than you usually do and see if it changes how you feel or act. If you are required to wear a uniform for your job, see if you can find a way to sneak in some aspect of your style, even if you're the only one who knows it's there.

My Living Space

The things that you have in your living space and the way it is decorated are other ways that you express who you are. As you make this list, think back to the bedrooms, dorm rooms, apartments, and/or homes you may have had throughout your life. What types of furniture did you choose (if you were the one who chose it)? What kinds of things did you have on your walls? What colors do you gravitate toward? Do you usually have more functional things or more decorative things? What type of flooring do you prefer? Do your spaces tend to be crowded or do they have more of a minimalist feel? If you could paint your walls any color, what colors would you choose? What type of lighting do you like? If you had unlimited resources, what changes would you make to your current living space?

Look over your list and then look around at your current living space. How much is your style incorporated into your current living space? If your current living space is not aligned with your style, play around with simple things that could help it align more (i.e., paint or change your lightbulbs, paint your furniture, tidy up a cluttered spot, create a little piece of art with colors you like, get a welcome mat, pick some flowers to put in a vase, etc.).

My Past

While I will always advocate for living in the present moment instead of dwelling too much on the past or trying to predict the future, the experiences you've had in your past can provide a lot of very important information about the things that have impacted and shaped you into who you are today. In going through this section, it might be helpful to pull out old photo albums or journals to help activate some of your memories, and it could also be helpful to talk to family members and/or friends you've had in your earlier years.

The lists you make in this section can deepen your understanding of who you have been, and can allow you to choose how much of that you want to carry forward.

Throughout this section, please remember that you are the creator of your path from this day on, and just because something was an important part of your past does not mean it needs to be part of your present and your future. This whole process is a bit like remodeling a house—you get to keep the things that work for you and replace the things that don't.

My Memories

This is intentionally a very broad topic, and this will be a list you will probably need to return to multiple times as different memories show up for you. Thinking back to your past, what are the moments, both big and small, that stand out to you? Just start writing whatever pops into your awareness.

If you're feeling stuck, it could be helpful to create a timeline and go through your life by 1-year, 5-year, or 10-year periods and ask yourself what stands out during that time. Think about experiences that happened in your home, your family, your friendships, your school, your city, your country, the world at large—what specific moments stand out in your mind as you let yourself travel back through your life?

Look through your list. Choose a few of your memories that have been very impactful for you, and spend some time with each one exploring how exactly it impacted you. What did you learn from it? What changed for you as a result of what happened? How might your life have been different if it would not have happened?

People Who Have Been Meaningful to Me

Think about the people from all different periods of your life who have impacted you in some way. Maybe it was the grandfather who taught you important life lessons or the kid who bullied you in third grade. Everyone in your path has played some sort of role in teaching you, guiding you, comforting you, hurting you, or even showing you the type of person you do or do not want to be. As you make your list, it might be helpful to write not only the name of the person who impacted you, but also a few words about how each person impacted you.

Look through your list. Is there anyone on the list you feel compelled to reach out to in order to express gratitude? Do it!

Things I've Overcome

Think about the struggles and challenges, both big and small, you've gotten yourself through and overcome throughout your life. Maybe you endured a job with a difficult boss, maybe you quit drinking or using drugs, maybe you stood up to a bully, or maybe you got through a difficult breakup. Everything you've overcome is something to be proud of and can help you reconnect with and build your confidence and resilience.

Look through your list and think about HOW you were able to overcome each of those things. What were the specific internal and external factors that contributed to your success? Knowing the "how" is the key to understanding your resilience and can help in overcoming current and future challenging situations.

Jobs

Look back through your life and make a list of all the different jobs you've had—the ones you've loved, the ones you've hated, and everything in between. Think beyond jobs you've been officially hired to do, and include volunteer work, chores at home, and any other duties and responsibilities you've had.

Once you've created your list, go back through it and make some notes. Which jobs did you really like or really not like, and what were the specific things about the job that you really liked or didn't like? Once you've identified these things, start to look for patterns in the types of things that really seem to feed your spirit and the types of things that are just not a good fit for you.

Regrets

While it's important not to spend too much energy dwelling on regrets, the things you regret can give you valuable guidance in how you want to move forward with your life. You can use the information about things you regret to a) find a way to remedy or do them differently if that's still a possibility, and b) be more intentional about living out your present life in such a way that when you look back on this period of your life, you do not have similar regrets. Regrets can also give you clues about the ways that your priorities have shifted since many of the things we regret have to do with things we didn't think were important at the time. Use this list to reflect on some of the things you regret doing or not doing throughout your life.

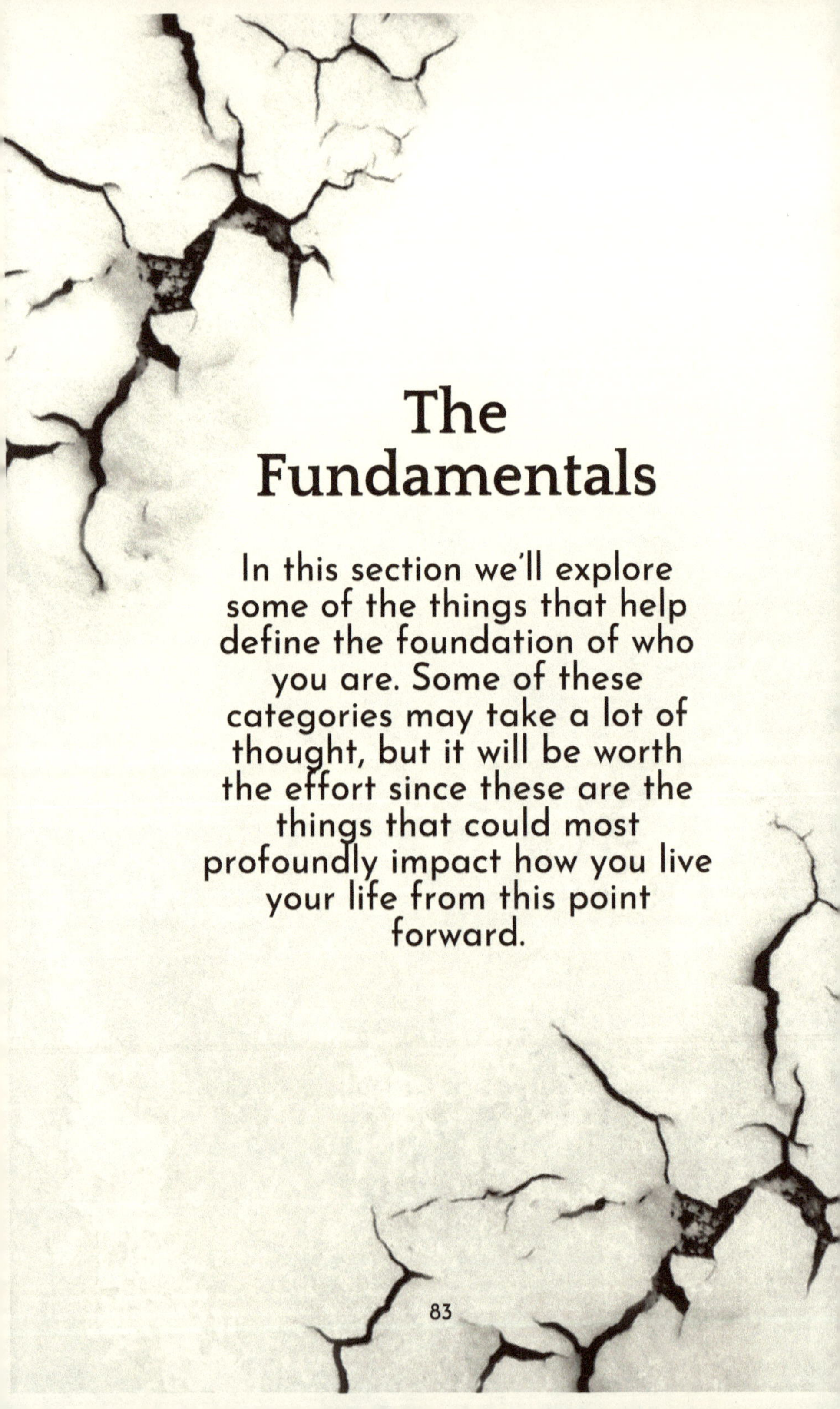

The Fundamentals

In this section we'll explore some of the things that help define the foundation of who you are. Some of these categories may take a lot of thought, but it will be worth the effort since these are the things that could most profoundly impact how you live your life from this point forward.

Things That Are Important to Me

Start by just creating a list of everything that comes to mind when you hear the question, "What's important to you?".

If you're feeling a little stuck, here are some of the things people tend to value: family, financial stability, power, physical health, mental health, personal growth, spirituality, adventure/travel, friendships, romantic relationships, pleasure, material possessions, creativity, work, freedom, rest, learning, integrity, etc.

Once you've made your initial list, spend some time going a little deeper and really exploring what you value in life. It could help to write each item from your list on strips of paper and put them in order of what you value most to what you value least.

It might also be helpful here to make a list of your ideal values and then another list of what someone looking in at your life from the outside might say that you value based on how you spend your time, energy, money, etc. And then just look and see how closely the two lists match up. If they are very similar, you're probably living in a way that aligns with what's important to you. If the two lists aren't very similar, it's just great information about some of the things you might be able to change so that you can be more aligned with what you value.

Another way you can use your list is to explore how some of the things you value might be at odds with each other in your current situation. For example, if financial stability is one of your top values and work is one of your lower values, you may experience some inner conflict if your job is currently your only way of making money. And it could get even more complicated if time with your family is also one of your top values, but you're working 80 hours a week so you can achieve financial stability.

This is all just great information that allows you to explore ideas and strategies for moving forward in a way that allows you to live more closely aligned with what's really important to you.

Things I Believe

Start by making a list of whatever comes into your mind when you hear the words, "What do you believe?" These can be big beliefs about things like what you think happens after you die or beliefs as simple as whether or not you think pineapple belongs on pizza.

If you're feeling a little stuck, here are some questions to get you started:

- ·People: Are people generally kind and trustworthy? Can people be rehabilitated if they have committed crimes? Do people usually get what they deserve"?
- ·Spirituality and Religion: Is there a higher power? What do you believe about forgiveness? Are the events of our lives predetermined? What happens after we die?
- ·Family/Relationships: What do you believe about traditional family roles? How much of a say should children have in family decisions? What do you believe about divorce?
- ·Politics: Which political party's beliefs are most similar to yours? What issues are important for politicians/government to address? What is the ideal ratio of government control vs personal freedom?
- ·Miscellaneous: What components are necessary for a fulfilling life? What is the ideal ratio of work/productivity to rest/play? Does pineapple belong on pizza?

This will definitely be a list that you'll want to return to as you have life experiences that might shape new beliefs and/or shift the beliefs you already have.

My Standards

Think about your standards in friendships, romantic relationships, work, your home, etc. Consider the factors that must be present for you to feel fulfilled and the dealbreakers that would cause you to walk away and find something different. It can also be helpful to think about any guidelines or rules you might have for yourself. For example, maybe you don't check work email while you're at home, maybe you don't drink when you're alone, maybe you try to exercise at least three days a week, etc.

Knowing more about your standards and personal guidelines can help you establish and maintain healthy boundaries and can help you be more deliberate with what you do. It will definitely be helpful to return to this list as life experiences teach you more about your needs and boundaries.

Spend some time reflecting on the standards you've written on your list. What experiences helped you create your current standards? How does it feel when you honor/stick to your standards? Are there any of your standards that create pushback from others? If so, what is this like for you and how do you handle it?

Be improbable,
something unexpected,
something unlikely,
something outrageous.
Surprise the world
with your determination,
your revolutionary passion,
your courage to do and be
anything you want, even
(and especially),
the things that are unlikely and
outrageous...

-from the poem
"Improbable""
by Emily Bowman

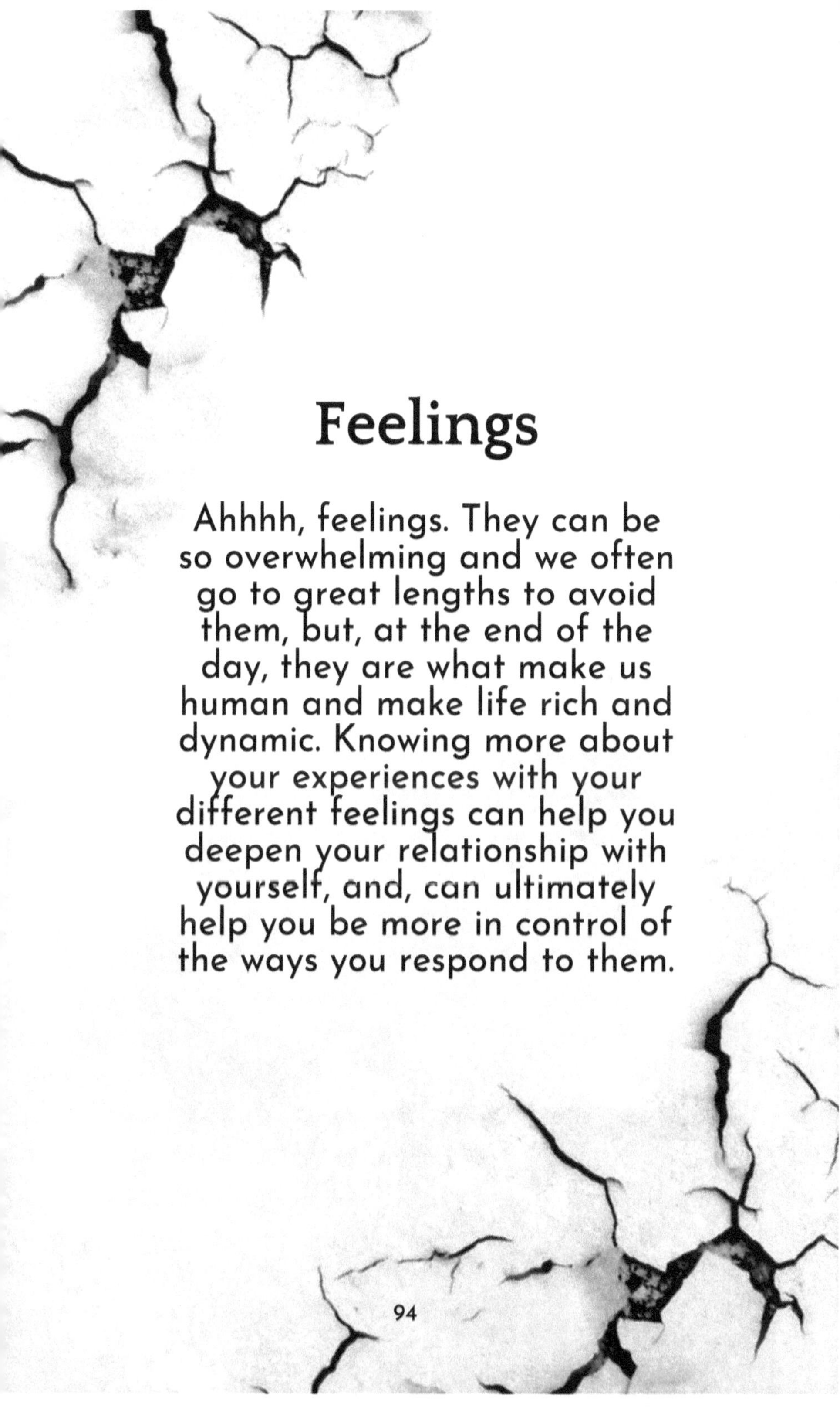

Feelings

Ahhhh, feelings. They can be so overwhelming and we often go to great lengths to avoid them, but, at the end of the day, they are what make us human and make life rich and dynamic. Knowing more about your experiences with your different feelings can help you deepen your relationship with yourself, and, can ultimately help you be more in control of the ways you respond to them.

Things That Bring Me Joy and Happiness

Begin by listing everything in your life right now that brings you joy. Then, think back throughout your life to the moments that have been most joyful. What were you doing? Who were you with? Where were you? What were you wearing? What was the weather like? These are all clues you can use to identify sources of joy and happiness. Then, once you've remembered how joyful joy feels and how happy happiness feels, you can start noticing these experiences in your current life, and your list will grow and grow.

Things I Feel Angry About

Some of you may be able to dive right in and make long, long lists in this category, and some of you may have a hard time coming up with anything at all. Simply noticing which category you fall into is great information about yourself, in and of itself! We all receive a lot of different, and often conflicting, messages about anger from our families, our cultural groups, and our society at large. If you are someone who has a hard time connecting with your anger, work with giving yourself permission to feel angry about things even if only for the purpose of making this list. And if the word "anger" feels too overwhelming for you, substitute any of anger's younger cousins (annoyance, frustration, irritation, etc.).

Ultimately, anger is about feeling like our limits are being pushed in some way, so once you have an idea about the types of things that usually result in anger for you, you will know more about what types of boundaries you might need to set. In many cases, though, even with boundaries in place, our limits will still get pushed. Knowledge is power, though, and knowing what activates your anger can help you be more in control of how you respond to it.

Things That Help Me Feel Calm

Hopefully making this list and thinking of the things that calm you will be a calming experience, in and of itself. Think about things you do that soothe you and calm you, things that help you slow down when your mind is going a million miles a minute, or things that bring you peace when life feels especially chaotic. If you're having a hard time starting this list and coming up with specific things that calm you, begin to simply notice how you feel when you're doing certain things, listening to certain songs, being around certain people, being in certain places, etc. You might also ask the people around you what's calming for them and try some of those things to see if any of them work for you.

Once you have at least a few items on your list, you may want to copy and post it somewhere you can see it regularly or access it easily when you're feeling overwhelmed or having a hectic day.

Things I Feel Sad About

Start by thinking about the last time you cried (sad-cried, not joy-cried). What were you feeling sad about? What types of things typically lead you to feel sad? Sadness is often about loss, so knowing the things you feel sad about can be another clue to what is important to you. Sadness can also be about pain, and it can acquaint you with some of your unresolved hurts and unmet needs.

Note: If your sadness feels more like a persistent depression than temporary sadness, it may be helpful to talk to a mental health professional.

Things I Worry About

We all have worries from time to time. Although the content of our worry changes depending on the specific things going on in our lives, we typically find ourselves stuck on certain themes of worry (relationships, health, work, existential questions, money, future, etc.). Start by writing down anything you're currently worrying about. It can be as simple as what you're going to make for dinner tonight, or as complex as whether or not you're living a meaningful life. Then, think back over your life to the things that have been on your mind most often or have repeatedly kept you awake at night. Have your worries changed over time or are you still worrying about the same types of things you were worrying about 20 years ago, 10 years ago, 5 years ago? Once you're aware of what your worry patterns tend to be, you have more insight into the things that are most important to you. You can also begin to take more control of your mind by acknowledging the worry thoughts as simply thoughts about things that are important to you, and then you get to decide how much time and energy you put into those thoughts, and whether or not they are helpful for you.

Note: If you are struggling with excessive worry thoughts and they are regularly interfering with your sleep, your work, your relationships, your health, etc., you may benefit from talking to a mental health professional.

Look over your list and circle the things you have control over or can impact in some way. For the things you didn't circle, you can decide whether you want to keep worrying about them or whether you want to use all the energy you'd usually spend worrying and put it toward something more constructive. For the things you did circle, you can decide how much energy you want/need to continue to put into worrying about them.

If you want to take this a step further, consider that worrying can be a way that we try to avoid being in our bodies and really feeling deeper feelings that might be uncomfortable and overwhelming. As you look at your list and think about your worry patterns in general, it could be helpful to ask yourself what deeper feelings your worries might be trying to protect you from.

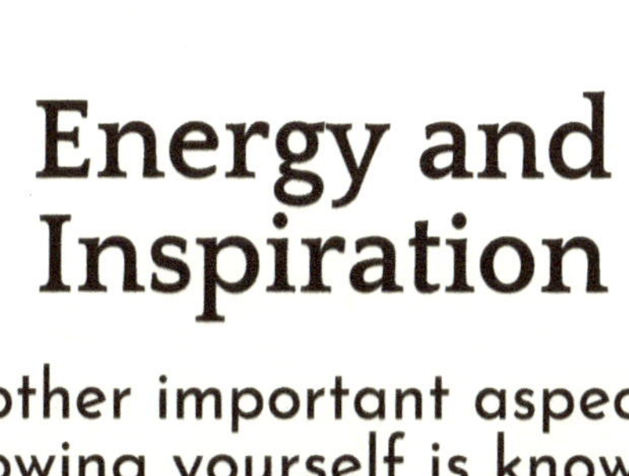

Energy and Inspiration

Another important aspect of knowing yourself is knowing more about what replenishes and what depletes your energy, as well as what inspires you. Knowing these things about yourself allows you to live a richer, more fulfilling, more creative, and more aligned life.

Things That Inspire Me

Don't limit yourself to just one form of inspiration when creating this list. You can be inspired in a number of ways. You can be inspired to be a better person or live a more fulfilling life, you can be inspired to achieve a goal or give to someone, and you can be inspired to build a business or create artistically. Think about the last time you felt inspired. What exactly was it that inspired you? Inspiration can come from books you read or things you watch. It can come from other people's examples or other people's words. It can come from nature or music or art or mystical experiences. It can also come from being still and connecting to your deepest desires and callings. Write down all the ways you've experienced inspiration throughout your life, and keep adding to this list as you find new forms of inspiration.

My Spirituality

Spirituality can mean a number of different things to people. For some people it is a sense that they are connected to something that feels bigger than themselves. For some people it is associated with a specific religion or practice. There is no correct or incorrect way to experience spirituality, there is simply your way, and this is your chance to explore what that means to you. Start by just answering the question, "What does spirituality mean to you?", then write down all the ways you practice and nourish your spirituality.

To deepen your understanding of your spirituality, it could be helpful to create a timeline to explore how your spirituality has evolved throughout your life, as well as the experiences and people and teachings that have shaped it.

Things That Energize Me

Think about the people, places, activities, experiences, music, food, weather, etc. that help you feel energized. If you're having trouble coming up with anything, or if you feel like you never have energy no matter what, start by simply paying attention throughout each day to your energy level and the factors that seem to increase it, even if it's only a tiny bit. Use this list to note those things and to continue exploring all the things that give you energy.

Look over your list and identify the things you might be able to do more often in order to add more energy into your life. Come up with a plan to implement at least one of those things in the next week.

Things That Leave Me Feeling Drained

Now, think about the people, places, activities, experiences, music, food, weather, etc. that tend to leave you feeling drained. If you're having trouble coming up with anything, start by just paying attention throughout each day to your energy level and the factors that seem to deplete it.

Look over your list and identify the things you might be able to eliminate, avoid, or do less often. For the things on your list that are unavoidable, think about how you might be able to balance your energy scale by pairing them with some of the things that give you energy. For example, if driving in heavy traffic is something that drains you, but you have to do it to get to work every day, you could balance it by listening to music that gives you energy while you drive.

People I Admire

Begin by writing the names of anyone who comes to mind when you hear the question, "Who do you admire?" These can be famous people, co-wokers, friends, family members, characters from books or movies, historical figures, etc. Don't censor, don't edit, just write. This will likely be a list to which you add frequently as you are introduced to new people throughout your life.

Once you have at least a few names on your list, go back to each name and spend some time contemplating what you admire about that person. Notice if there are any patterns in the things you tend to admire about people. Sometimes the things we admire in others can be the characteristics and behaviors we most desire, and other times they can be characteristics and behaviors of ourselves that we either can't see or have suppressed in some way. This list can be a valuable tool in understanding yourself more fully and in creating the life you want as you move forward.

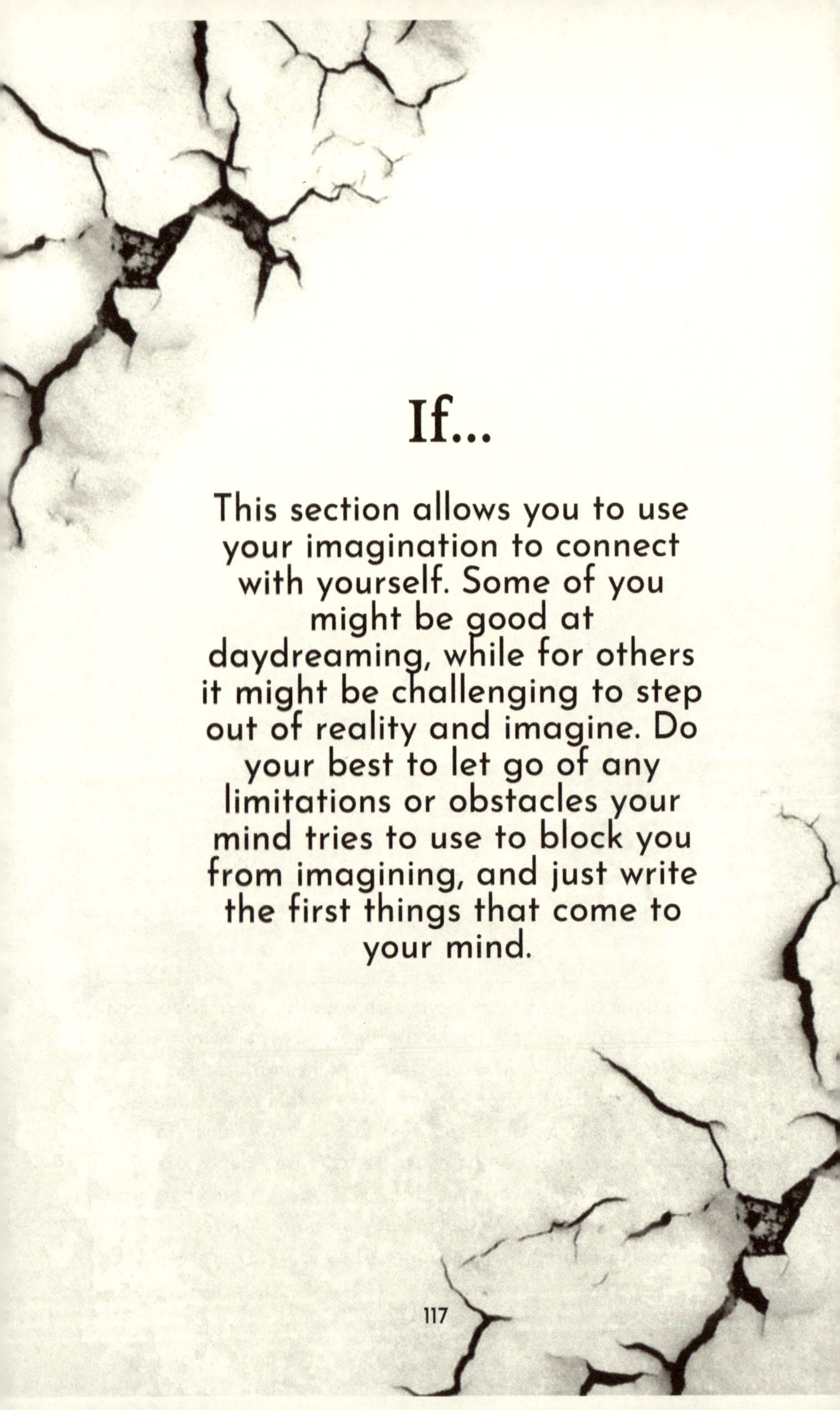

If...

This section allows you to use your imagination to connect with yourself. Some of you might be good at daydreaming, while for others it might be challenging to step out of reality and imagine. Do your best to let go of any limitations or obstacles your mind tries to use to block you from imagining, and just write the first things that come to your mind.

If I Had a Day, a Weekend, a Month, or a Year Off, I Would...

Start with a day...if you had a day off with nothing to do, nowhere to be, no one to answer to, what would you do? How about an entire weekend? A month? A year? Start by just writing the first things that come to mind, and then you can expand your list as you allow yourself to deepen into your imagination.

Once you've made your lists, look them over and compare them to how you spend your time currently. Is there anything that could change so that the way you spend your time aligns more closely with your desires?

If I Had a Lot of Money, I Would...

If you inherited a big sum of money or won it in the lottery, how would you spend it? How much of it would you spend on things vs experiences? How much would you spend on yourself vs others? How much of it would you save or invest? There are no right or wrong answers, just write anything that pops into your mind. This list can be valuable in helping you flesh out your values, and it can also help you explore your current relationship with money and beliefs about money.

Dream Jobs

If you could start working at any job in the world tomorrow without having to go through any sort of training or schooling, without having to move or disrupt your life in any way, what would it be? What are other jobs you've fantasized about having?

Once you have a list of dream jobs, look it over and ask yourself what obstacles are currently standing between you and those jobs. You might also want to think about what appeals to you about those jobs, and whether or not there might be ways to do something similar through a hobby or volunteer work, or even a similar job.

Things I've Always Wanted to Try

What are some of the activities, hobbies, sports, artistic endeavors, instruments, etc. you've always wanted to try? When you were a child, what kinds of lessons did you wish you could take? What sports or clubs did you wish you could participate in? Throughout your life, what classes or community groups have sounded fun or interesting? When you hear people talking about their hobbies and interests, which ones spark your interest?

Look over your list and choose one thing that you could see yourself trying in the next six months. Do some research and figure out the steps you need to take to make it happen, and then...make it happen!

Places I Want to Go

Where have you always wanted to go? If someone gave you round-trip tickets to anywhere in the world, where would be some of the places you might choose? What places have you been to before and want to return? What historical landmarks or geographical features have you always wanted to experience?

Experiences I Want to Have

Maybe you want to swim with dolphins or play bass in a punk band. Maybe your dream experiences involve standing on top of a mountain or marching in a protest. Think about things you've read about or seen in movies, as well as things your friends and coworkers have done that tug at you a little when you hear about them. Be daring and outrageous with this list. Write down anything and everything you've had even an inkling of a desire to do.

Look over your list and choose one experience that might be possible in the next year. Do some research and figure out the steps you need to take to make it happen, and then...make it happen!

What I Want to See when I Look Back at My Life in Five Years

We all take backward glances at our lives from time to time. Think about what you want to see in a backward glance you might take five years from now. What do you want to be proud of? What do you want to stand out as important to you during that time? How do want to see that you've spent your time? What specific things do you want to have accomplished? What routines and habits do you want to have put into place? What do you not want to see?

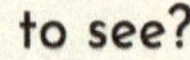

Look over your list and choose one of the things you want to see when you look back at your life five years from now. Spend some time thinking about what you might need to do to make it a reality, and then write out a little plan for yourself and put it into action!

Goals

All of the other lists in this section can help you with this list. Goals can be a little overwhelming and can feel a bit daunting, but they don't have to be. Basically a goal is just something specific you want to do or change, and the more specific you can be about it, the easier it will be to conceptualize it and come up with the steps you might need to take to achieve it. There's a common format people often use when setting goals and it goes by the acronym **SMART**. The 'S' stands for **Specific**.

The best goals are also easily **Measurable**. For example, you might have an overall goal of being "healthier", but what does that even mean? Maybe you'll measure it by being able to walk up the stairs without losing your breath, maybe you'll go to the gym at least three days a week, maybe your blood pressure will be lower.

It's also important for goals to be reasonably **Achievable**. A goal of making 10 million dollars in the next year, for example, is likely not reasonably achievable unless you have a very rich relative who leaves you all their money, you happen to stumble upon a great investment, or you already have a multi-million dollar job. A more achievable goal might be to increase your income by 10 percent.

The best goals are also those that are **Relevant** to your life. If you set a goal of becoming a movie star but have no intention of studying acting or moving to Hollywood to pursue a career in acting, that goal probably isn't very relevant to your life.

It can also be helpful for goals to be **Time-limited** so that you give yourself some parameters around when you want to accomplish them. You're more likely to accomplish a goal of starting guitar lessons by the end of the month than a goal of learning how to play the guitar before you die. Placing time limits on goals can create the sense of urgency that we all need when we are trying to get something done.

To start this list, maybe think about one SMART goal you can set for yourself in the next month, one in the next year, and one in the next five years. The fewer goals you have, the more likely you will be able to give each one a good amount of attention and energy, and the more likely you are to accomplish them. Setting a whole bunch of goals at once often leads to feeling overwhelmed, giving up, and then feeling like a "failure". Set yourself up for a positive experience with your goals!

Anything Else That Feels Important to Write Down

This book has covered several different ways you can connect with yourself in order to live a more intentional life, but there are certainly many, many more. If other ideas, topics, aspects of yourself, etc. have come to mind as you've been going through this book, please create as many of your own lists as you can!

This List is Called:

This List is Called:

This List is Called:

This List is Called:

This List is Called:

This List is Called:

Ideas for Further Exploration

In going through this book, you've hopefully gotten reacquainted with some foundational aspects of yourself, and gotten acquainted with new parts of yourself. While awareness and insight are wonderful things, and are, in and of themselves, valuable, it can be hard to figure out what to do with them, especially if you're a person who is oriented toward action. Here are some suggestions if you want to take this process further:

- Write a mission statement. Most companies and organizations have mission statements that reflect their core values and guide their missions. Thinking about what you know about your own values and what makes life meaningful for you, write a statement that can help guide you in living a more intentional life that aligns with who you really are and what you believe about your purpose.

- Write letters to yourself at different stages of your life. From your current vantage point, give your younger self the wisdom and advice you might have needed at that time. Then, write a letter to your current self from an older and wiser version of yourself. Give yourself feedback about the life you're living, and also give yourself some wisdom and advice about moving forward with your life.

- Create a piece of art (painting, collage, song, play, poem, piece of jewelry, etc.) that encapsulates all the things that make you who you are.

- Ask a friend or family member to take photos of you being as you as possible. Keep these photos as a reminder of who you really are.

- Write your ideal obituary. This may sound morbid, but it's actually a great way to reflect on the things that are important to you and the legacy you want to leave behind when it's time to go.

- Create a list of "Things I'm Learning about Myself" and make a practice of adding to it on a daily basis.

- Document your life. Write a memoir, make a film, write a play, etc. about the unique and important aspects of your life.

- Give to the world. Now that you know more about your specific talents, gifts, passions, and ideals, you can use them to contribute to the world through volunteer work, a job, a fundraiser, a donation, etc.

Closing Thoughts

I hope your journey through this book has been meaningful, and I hope the prompts have allowed you to remember important things about yourself and learn new things about yourself as you make the return to your own front door. Move forward with a greater sense of presence and purpose, and live your life in a more intentional, more aligned, more fulfilling way!

If this book has been meaningful to you, and if you feel inclined to share about the specific ways in which it has been meaningful, please do! I would absolutely LOVE to hear about your experiences and any feedback/ideas for future books. Feel free to email me at emilybowmanlpc@gmail.com. If you want to use social media to share your experiences with this process, you can use the hashtag #yourownfrontdoor to connect with others who are using the lists.

About the Author

Emily Bowman lives in Western Colorado. She has been a therapist for over 20 years, and she is passionate about guiding people on their paths of healing and growth. Emily is also a writer and engages in a number of other creative pursuits. Her experiences as a therapist, as well as her own experiences with growth and healing have given her valuable insights and inspiration as she explores the beauty and complexity of being human through her art.

In addition to *Your Own Front Door*, Emily has also written *reflect & expand*, a collection of original poems, photographs, and prompts for reflection and growth. Please visit www.sweetmoonpress for books, bookmarks, and cards created by Emily.

Acknowledgements

First and foremost, I'd like to express gratitude to my parents, Mike and Steph, for the wonderful, enthusiastic support of all of the projects and endeavors I've undertaken throughout my life, including this one. Your editorial help and feedback has been so valuable throughout the process of putting this project together. I'd also like to thank Benny BoOM for being such a creative, supportive partner and for inspiring me daily to turn my ideas into a reality I can share with the world. Thank you also to everyone who weighed in on the "lines vs no lines" debate...you gave great feedback and great ideas, and I am much appreciative. A special thank you to all of my clients through the years who have given me the honor of being present for your healing and growth, and who have taught me so many of the things that are necessary in this process of reconnecting with ourselves. And, of course, thank you to everyone who has ever said, "I don't know who I am"...you showed me the need to bring this book into the world, and I hope you are all able to eventually find your way back to your own front doors.

www.ingramcontent.com/pod-product-compliance
Lightning Source LLC
Chambersburg PA
CBHW030318160726
47992CB00005B/2067